How do I use this scheme?

Key Words with Peter and Jane has three
parallel series, each containing twelve books. All three
series are written using the same carefully controlled
vocabulary. Readers will get the most out of **Key Words** with
Peter and Jane when they follow the books in the pattern
1a, 1b, 1c; 2a, 2b, 2c and so on.

• Series a
gradually introduces and repeats new words.

• Series b
provides further practice of these same words, but
in a different context and with different illustrations.

• Series c
uses familiar words to teach **phonics** in a methodical way,
enabling children to read increasingly difficult words.
It also provides a link to writing.

LADYBIRD BOOKS

UK | USA | Canada | Ireland | Australia
India | New Zealand | South Africa

Ladybird Books is part of the Penguin Random House group of companies
whose addresses can be found at global.penguinrandomhouse.com.

www.penguin.co.uk   www.puffin.co.uk   www.ladybird.co.uk

Penguin
Random House
UK

First published 1964
This edition 2009, 2014, 2016
Copyright © Ladybird Books Ltd, 1964
001

A CIP catalogue record for this book is
available from the British Library

ISBN: 978-1-409-30116-5

Printed in China

Key Words

with Peter and Jane

4a

Things we do

written by W. Murray
illustrated by J.H. Wingfield

Peter and Jane are at home.

They want to make a car to play with. They want to make a car like Daddy's.

Jane helps Peter. "It looks good," she says. "We can have fun with it."

"I want to make it red," says Peter.

"Yes," says Jane, "we can make it red. You and I like red."

new words
make   she

5

Jane likes to help Mummy. She wants to make cakes like Mummy.

"Let me help you, Mummy," she says. "Will you let me help, please? I can make cakes like you."

"Yes," says Mummy, "I will let you help me. You are a good girl."

"We will make some cakes for Peter and Daddy," says Jane. "They like the cakes we make."

new words
Let let will

Peter and Jane like to draw. "Let us draw," says Jane. "I will draw you, Peter," she says.

"Yes, let us draw," says Peter. "I will draw a tree."

"Here you are, Peter," says Jane. "Here is Pat, and here is a ball. I will make the ball red. Come and look, Peter, come and look at this dog."

new words

draw   us

9

"I will draw," says Peter. "I like to draw. Look, Jane, look at this tree," he says. "I will draw a house in the tree. See this house."

"Let us make a house in a tree, Jane," says Peter. "Will Daddy let us? Will he let us make a house in a tree?"

"Yes, Peter," she says. "He will help us make it."

new word

house

Daddy lets the children have a house in a tree. He draws the house, and helps the children to make it.

"It will be a good house," says Peter. "It will be a good house for us to play in."

"Yes," says Jane, "it will be fun to play in it. Look, Pat wants to come up with us."

new words
children be

The children are in the house in the tree. The dog is with the children.

"Let us have tea here," says Jane. "That will be fun," she says.

"Yes," says Peter, "you make the tea. I will draw. I will draw some flowers."

"Yes, I will get the tea," says Jane. "I like to get the tea."

no new words

15

The children are on the bus. Pat is with the children. He wants to jump up with Jane.

"No," says Jane to the dog. "Get off, Pat. Get off. Be a good dog."

"Look," says Peter. "There go the Police. There is a Police car. Can you see, Jane? There they go."

"Yes," says Jane, "here are the shops. Let us get off here."

new words

off There there

bus stop
ILX HABDUNG
WAINICA

POLICE

17

The children get off the bus, then they go off to the shops.

"Let us shop for Mummy, then we can look at the sweets and toys," says Jane. "There is the fish shop," she says. "We have to get fish."

"Yes," says Peter. "You get the fish. I will get apples and cakes."

The children go into the shops.

---

new word

then

The children are at home. They make a shop. "I will be the man in the shop," says Peter.

"Then let me be Mummy," Jane says. "I want some things for the house," she says, "and then I want

some things for tea. Give me some flowers, please, and I want some apples."

Peter puts in the flowers and the apples. "There you are," he says.

new words
things **puts**

The children have to work.

Peter has to help Daddy work with the car. Jane has to help Mummy work in the house. She and Peter like to help Mummy work.

"It is good to work, and it is good to play," says Mummy. "Let us put the play things away, and then water the flowers. Then we will make the beds," she says.

new words
work   away

Peter is at work with his daddy. He and Jane like to work with Daddy.

"Go away," he says to Pat. "Go away. Be off with you. I want to work."

Daddy says, "Put the things down there, and then help me make a fire."

Peter puts his things down. "Good," he says. "I want to make a fire."

new words
his   fire

Peter helps his Daddy to make a big fire.

"I like this work," says Peter.

"It is like play," says Jane. "Put some things on the fire. Daddy wants a big fire."

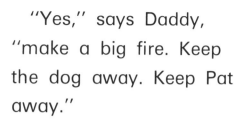

"Yes," says Daddy, "make a big fire. Keep the dog away. Keep Pat away."

"Come here, Pat," says Jane. "Come to me. Be a good dog and keep away."

new words
big   Keep   keep

You can see Daddy at his big fire.

The children like to play with water. Jane has a little boat and Peter has a big boat. Pat wants to play with Peter's big boat.

"Keep Pat away," says Peter to Jane. "He wants my boat. He wants my big boat."

"Come here, Pat," says Jane. "You can have my ball to play with."

new words

little   my

The two children are in the water. They want to fish.

Peter has a fish. "Look at my big one," he says.

"Will you keep it?" says Jane.

"No," he says. Peter puts his big fish into the water.

Jane says, "Look, I have two little ones." She puts her fish into the water. She puts her two little ones in.

"Off they go," Jane says.

---

new words

two   her

The two children are at the farm.
They want to help at the farm.
They like to work there.

Here they are with the horses.

Jane likes her little horse. She gives it an apple. She wants to keep her little horse.

Peter has a big horse. "I want to get on my horse, Jane," he says. "Help me up, please."

new words
farm   horse

Jane helps Peter to get on his big horse. "There you are," she says. "Away you go."

"Thank you," says Peter. "Thank you, Jane."

Then Jane gets on her little horse.

"Away I go, on my horse,"
she says.

The two children go off to work
on the farm.

"Let us help with the cows," says
Peter.

"Yes," says Jane, "we will help
with the cows."

new words
Thank   thank   cows

"Let us help the man milk the cows," says Jane. "Will he let us help him milk?" she says.

"Yes," says Peter, "he likes us to help him with his work."

"Can we help you?" says Peter.

"Thank you," says the man. "Yes, please. You two can help me with the milk. Put the horses away. Come in and help me with the cows."

| new words |
| milk   him |

The two children play at home.

"What will you do?" says Peter.

"I will make a toy farm," Jane says. "What will you do, Peter?"

"I want to help you make the farm," he says.

"Thank you," says Jane.

"The farm house was there," she says. "Here is the big horse and my little horse. Let the man milk his cows. Keep the dog away. Put him with the horses."

Jane likes cats. She has a little cat.

"What do you want?" she says to her cat. "Do you want some milk?"

"The cows on the farm give good milk," says Jane. "I will give her some."

Peter comes in with his big rabbit. "What is that, Jane?" he says. "Is it milk? Give some to my rabbit, please."

"Thank you," he says. "Keep the cat away."

---

new word

cat

The children, Daddy and Mummy all go to the sea. Here they all are in the train at the station.

The cat and the dog are at home.

Jane says, "Away we all go to the sea. What can we do at the sea, Daddy?"

"You can all do what you like," Daddy says to her.

Peter says, "We can go in a boat, and play in the water."

new words

all   sea

Here they all are at the sea. The children can do what they like. They can go into the sea, play games, or fish, or be with Mummy and Daddy.

"Play a game with us, Daddy," says Peter.

"Yes, play a game, please," says Jane.

Daddy says he will play a game with the big ball.

"Good," says Jane. "It is fun to play games with him."

The two children like to play games. The cat looks on.

Peter says, "Do you want to play with my toys or play at schools?"

"Let us play at schools," says Jane. "What will you do, read or draw?"

"I want to read," says Peter. "All children like to read."

"Read this," says Jane. "Read this, Peter."

Peter reads. "It says DANGER," he says. "I can read DANGER."

"Yes, it is DANGER," Jane says.

---

new words

read   DANGER

Jane's cat is not big. She likes to go up the tree for a game.

"Stop her," says Jane. "She gets up the tree and can not get down. Stop her, Peter. Please stop her."

Peter can not stop the cat. "She can not get down," he says. "There is no danger. You or I can get her, or we can get Daddy to help."

"No," says Jane, "all we have to do is get some milk."

The cat sees the milk and then comes down.

---

new words

not Stop stop

Daddy, Mummy, Jane, Peter and Pat are all here. The cat is at home.

"Look," says Peter. "There is DANGER, STOP. I can read DANGER, STOP."

Jane says, "I can read TO THE SEA and TO THE STATION."

Daddy says, "Yes, that is good. You can read."

Jane says to Pat, "Come here. You are not to jump up at the car. It is not Daddy's car."

"Let us all go home to tea," says Mummy.

"Yes," says Daddy, "we will all go home."

no new words

New words used in this book

Total number of new words: 42
Average repetition per word: 13